A Bear's Tale

THIS EDITION
Editorial Management by Oriel Square
Produced for DK by WonderLab Group LLC
Jennifer Emmett, Erica Green, Kate Hale, *Founders*

Editor Maya Myers; **Photography Editor** Nicole DiMella; **Managing Editor** Rachel Houghton;
Designers Project Design Company; **Researcher** Michelle Harris;
Copy Editor Lori Merritt; **Indexer** Connie Binder; **Proofreader** Susan K. Hom;
Authenticity Reader Dr. Naomi R. Caldwell; **Series Reading Specialist** Dr. Jennifer Albro

First American Edition, 2024
Published in the United States by DK Publishing, a division of Penguin Random House LLC
1745 Broadway, 20th Floor, New York, NY 10019

Copyright © 2024 Dorling Kindersley Limited
25 26 27 10 9 8 7 6 5 4 3
003-339658-Apr/2024

All rights reserved.
Without limiting the rights under the copyright reserved above, no part of this publication may be reproduced, stored in or introduced into a retrieval system, or transmitted, in any form, or by any means (electronic, mechanical, photocopying, recording, or otherwise), without the prior written permission of the copyright owner. Published in Great Britain by Dorling Kindersley Limited

A catalog record for this book is available from the Library of Congress.
HC ISBN 978-0-7440-9424-4
PB ISBN 978-0-7440-9398-8

DK books are available at special discounts when purchased in bulk for sales promotions, premiums, fund-raising, or educational use. For details, contact:
DK Publishing Special Markets, 1745 Broadway, 20th Floor, New York, NY 10019
SpecialSales@dk.com

Printed and bound in China

Super Readers Lexile® levels BR40 to 300L Lexile® is the registered trademark of MetaMetrics, Inc.
Copyright © 2023 MetaMetrics, Inc. All rights reserved.

The publisher would like to thank the following for their kind permission to reproduce their images: a=above; c=center; b=below; l=left; r=right; t=top; b/g=background
Alamy Stock Photo: All Canada Photos / Bob Gurr 16-17, All Canada Photos / Dave Blackey 8-9, All Canada Photos / Stephen J. Krasemann 17bc, Design Pics Inc / Alaska Stock RF / Doug Lindstrand 7br, 20bc, Design Pics Inc / Wave Royalty Free, Inc. 13br, 23clb, FLPA 20crb, Rolf Hicker Photography 3, Jason O. Watson (USA: Alaska photographs) 8bc, Westend61 GmbH / Fotofeeling 16bc, 23la **Bridgeman Images:** Gift Of Elizabeth H. Penn 9bl; **Dreamstime.com:** David Burke 19br, Antonio Guillem 12-13, 14-15, Klomsky 1, Derrick Neill 7bc, Ovydyborets 19bl, Joe Sohm 9br, Wirestock 11b, Maria Zebroff 18bc; **Getty Images:** Moment / Colleen Gara 4-5, 23cl, Moment / Jared Lloyd 6-7, Photodisc / Don Grall 10-11, 23bl, Stone / Paul Souders 14bc, 15bl, 15bc, The Image Bank / Mark Newman 13bl, 20-21, Universal Images Group / Education Images 18-19; **Getty Images / iStock:** Jillian Cooper 22, 23tl, DigitalVision Vectors / mecaleha 4bl, 6bc, llvllagic 10bc; **Shutterstock.com:** EVGENNI 21b, saraporn 17br; **VectorStock:** renreeser 12bc

Cover images: *Front:* **Dreamstime.com:** Anastasiya Aheyeva;
Back: **Dreamstime.com:** Pavel Naumov cb; **Getty Images / iStock:** PCH-Vector cra

www.dk.com

Pre-level

A Bear's Tale

Alli Brydon

Summer begins.
A grizzly bear walks
on four feet.
The bear walks
in its home.
Its home is
the woods.

The bear is big.
The bear is strong.

fur

claws

It can stay alive in the wild.

People honor the bear. They think bears are brave and smart.

art

People make art about bears. They tell stories about them.

woods

People stay away from the bear. This is also a way they honor it. The grizzly walks in the woods alone.

mountain

marks

The bear marks a tree. The marks tell other bears to stay away.

fight

But if another bear comes, the bears fight. The bear is hurt, but it stays strong.

The air turns cool in fall. Soon, it will be winter. The bear digs a den.

den

It will rest here for the winter. First, the bear must fill its belly.

The bear hunts for fish to eat. People also hunt fish.

The bear picks berries. People also eat berries.

fish

19

It is winter.
The woods are cold.
There is little food
to eat.
It is time for the bear
to rest.
It goes in its den.

rest

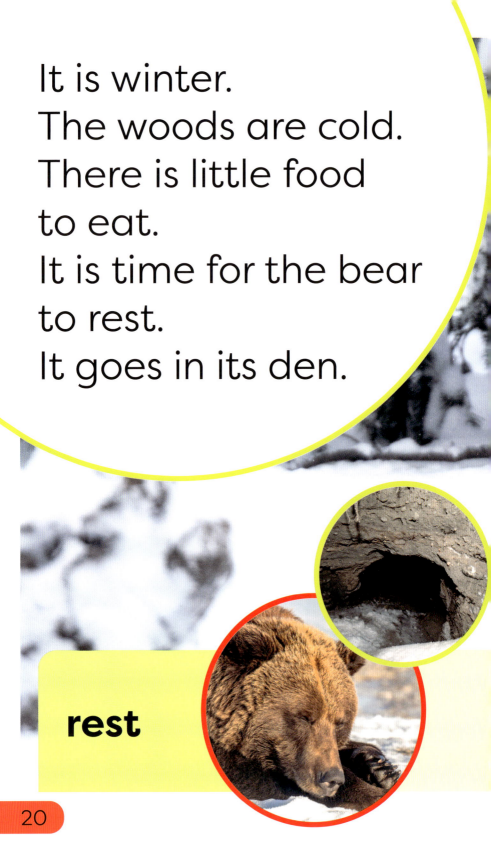

21

Spring comes.
The bear has cubs!
Now, there are more bears.
The bears walk in the forest.
Soon, it will be summer again.

Glossary

cubs
baby bears

den
a cave or place bears dig for shelter

grizzly bear
a large kind of bear

marks
indentations left by something

woods
forest

Quiz

Answer the questions to see what you have learned. Check your answers with an adult.

1. Where do grizzly bears live?
2. How do people honor bears?
3. How can a bear tell other animals to stay away?
4. What are some foods that bears eat?
5. Where does a bear rest during the winter?

1. Woods 2. Through art and stories 3. By marking trees
4. Fish and berries 5. In a den